Guided Autogenic Training

Mindfulness Exercise for Reducing Arousal, Deep Relaxation, Reduce Stress and Feel at Peace

By

DAPHNE KILLIAN

This book is dedicated to my two lovely daughters Anna and Bella for their support and encouragement.

TABLE OF CONTENTS

Chapter 1: Introduction to Guided Autogenic Training: Understanding the Benefits and Science Behind This Mindfulness Technique

Chapter 2: The Power of Breathing: Techniques for Achieving Deep Relaxation and Reducing Arousal

Chapter 3: Progressive Muscle Relaxation: A Step-by-Step Guide to Relieving Tension and Stress in Your Body

Chapter 4: Visualizing Peace and Tranquility: Harnessing the Power of Your Imagination to Promote Deep Relaxation

Chapter 5: Use imagery: As you practice PMR, you can also use imagery to enhance your relaxation. For example, imagine yourself in a peaceful setting, like a beach or forest, and focus on the sounds and sensations of that environment.

Chapter 6: Achieving Mental Clarity and Focus: Techniques for Clearing Your Mind and Eliminating Distractions

chapter 7: Understanding and Overcoming Negative Thought Patterns: Strategies for Developing a Positive Mindset

chapter 8: Mindfulness Meditation: Achieving Inner Peace and Tranquility Through Focused Attention

chapter 9: Cultivating Gratitude and Appreciation: Techniques for Recognizing and Celebrating the Good Things in Your Life

chapter 10: Applying Guided Autogenic Training in Your Daily Life: Incorporating These Mindfulness Techniques Into Your Daily Routine for Lasting Results.

Chapter 1

Introduction to Guided Autogenic Training: Understanding the Benefits and Science Behind This Mindfulness Technique

It can be tough to find moments of calm and relaxation in our fast-paced and demanding environment. As a result of the continual pressure and stress that modern life may bring, many people suffer from anxiety, depression, and other mental health disorders. Fortunately, there are effective solutions available to assist folks in dealing with stress and achieving greater levels of peace and tranquillity in their life. Guided Autogenic Training is one such tool, a mindfulness practice used by millions of people worldwide to produce deep relaxation, reduce alertness, and remove stress.

What is the definition of Guided Autogenic Training?

Guided Autogenic Training is a mindfulness technique created by German psychiatrist Johannes Heinrich Schultz in the 1920s. The technique consists of a series of exercises that encourage profound relaxation and aid in the attainment of inner peace and tranquillity. The practice is founded on the premise that the body and mind are inextricably linked, and that by encouraging relaxation in the body, people can reach higher levels of mental and emotional well-being.

The approach is known as "autogenic" because it promotes relaxation by self-generated ideas, also known as "autosuggestions." These instructions are often repeated slowly and deliberately, either quietly or aloud, with the goal of assisting the client in achieving a state of deep relaxation and tranquility.

What Is the Process of Guided Autogenic Training?

Guided Autogenic Training promotes deep relaxation in both the body and psyche. When we are stressed or anxious, our bodies respond by releasing stress hormones like cortisol and adrenaline. These hormones can create physical symptoms like increased heart rate, fast breathing, and muscle tightness, which can exacerbate stress and anxiety.

Through a series of relaxation exercises, Guided Autogenic Training assists individuals in reducing these physical signs of stress and anxiety. Typically, these exercises entail focusing on different parts of the body and repeating autosuggestions aimed to encourage relaxation and lessen tension.

One exercise might be to concentrate on the muscles in the arms and repeat the autosuggestion "my arms are heavy and warm." Individuals can induce relaxation and reduce muscle tension by focusing on the sensations of warmth and heaviness in their arms.

Guided Autogenic Training: The Science Behind It

While Guided Autogenic Training has been utilized for than a century to induce relaxation and stress reduction, scientists have just recently began to investigate the technique in greater depth. According to research, Guided Autogenic Training can be a highly effective strategy for inducing relaxation and reducing stress, with long-term advantages.

Individuals who followed Guided Autogenic Training for four weeks, for example, showed significant reductions in symptoms of sadness, anxiety, and tension, according to one study. Another study discovered that the approach was beneficial in lowering post-traumatic stress disorder (PTSD) symptoms in combat veterans.

Guided Autogenic Training has also been shown to improve physical health by lowering blood pressure and enhancing sleep quality. The approach has even been shown to be useful in lowering pain levels in people suffering from chronic pain.

How to Begin with Guided Autogenic Training

If you want to undertake Guided Autogenic Training for yourself, there are several tools to help you get started. Many therapists and mental health professionals provide guided sessions in the technique, and there are also a variety of books and online resources available to assist you learn it on your own.

When first beginning out with Guided Autogenic Training, keep in mind that the technique requires experience and patience. While some people may notice instant benefits from the approach, others may need to practice for weeks or even months before they notice major improvements in their mental and emotional well-being. It is also critical to approach the technique with an open and curious mind, and to be willing to experiment with many techniques and variants to find what works best for you.

The necessity of relaxing is one of the most crucial things to remember when doing Guided Autogenic Training. This entails finding a quiet and comfortable place where you may rest without distractions and focusing on your breathing and physiological sensations.

Many people find that practicing Guided Autogenic Training in the morning or evening, when they have some uninterrupted time to focus on themselves, is beneficial. However, the technique can be used at any time of day and is especially beneficial at times of extreme stress or anxiety.

It can be beneficial to begin your Guided Autogenic Training practice with easy exercises that focus on promoting calm in the body. Begin by focusing on the sensations of warmth and heaviness in your arms and repeating the autosuggestion "my arms are heavy and warm." As you gain confidence in the method, you can try more complex exercises that target other sections of the body and produce deeper levels of relaxation.

Conclusion

Guided Autogenic Training is a strong strategy for increasing relaxation, decreasing agitation, and improving mental and emotional well-being. While the procedure has been available for than a century, experts have only recently began to investigate its benefits in greater depth. Guided

Autogenic Training has been demonstrated in studies to be highly successful in reducing feelings of depression, anxiety, and stress, as well as having physical health advantages such as lowering blood pressure and enhancing sleep quality.

If you want to undertake Guided Autogenic Training for yourself, there are several tools to help you get started. Whether you work with a mental health professional or study the technique on your own, the most important thing is to approach it with an open and inquiring mind, as well as to be patient and persistent in your practice. Guided Autogenic Training can help you acquire greater levels of serenity, tranquility, and well-being in your life with time and practice.

Chapter 2

The Power of Breathing: Techniques for Achieving Deep Relaxation and Reducing Arousal

profound breathing techniques, which can help to lower arousal and induce profound relaxation in the body, are an important component of Guided Autogenic Training. Breathing is an essential part of our physiology, and learning to control our breath allows us to have more control over our mental and emotional states.

In this chapter, we will look at some of the most successful breathing techniques for establishing deep relaxation and lowering arousal, as well as how these techniques can be included into your Guided Autogenic Training practice.

The Advantages of Deep Breathing

Before we get into the exact deep breathing techniques, it's crucial to understand why this practice is so effective. When we take deep breaths, we activate the parasympathetic nerve system, which regulates our bodies' rest and digest processes. This activation causes a decrease in heart rate, blood pressure, and muscle tension, as well as a reduction in anxiety and promotes feelings of relaxation and well-being.

Deep breathing has been found to provide a variety of mental and physical health advantages, including:

- Reducing anxiety and depression symptoms
- Boosting immunological function

- Enhancing cognitive function and mental clarity by increasing energy levels
- Inflammation reduction and healing promotion

Now that we've established the advantages of deep breathing, let's look at some particular strategies for implementing it into your Guided Autogenic Training.

Deep Breathing Strategies

There are numerous deep breathing techniques, and the most effective one will be determined by your own tastes and needs. Here are some of the most popular breathing techniques for reaching deep relaxation:

Breathing Diaphragmatically

Diaphragmatic breathing, often known as belly breathing or deep breathing, is inhaling deeply into the lower lungs. Lay on your back or sit in a comfortable position with your feet flat on the ground to practice this technique. Put one hand on your chest and one on your stomach. Focus on expanding your abdomen and feeling your hand rise as you inhale deeply through your nose. Slowly exhale through your mouth, allowing your belly to deflate and your hand to fall.

Breathing in a box

Box breathing is a technique that entails breathing in for a count, holding the breath for a count, exhaling for a count, and then holding the breath for another count. To practice this technique, sit in a comfortable position and take four deep breaths. Hold your breath for four counts, then exhale for four counts. Hold your breath for a count of four before repeating the cycle.

Breathing from the Other Nostril

Nadi Shodhana, or alternate nostril breathing, is a breathing method that involves breathing through one nostril at a time. Sit in a comfortable posture and place your right thumb over your right nostril to perform this technique. Inhale deeply via your left nostril, then close it with your ring finger and exhale through your right nose. Inhale via your right nostril, then close it with your thumb and exhale through your left nose. Rep the cycle, inhaling and exhaling from alternate nostrils.

4-7-8 Deep Breathing

4-7-8 breathing is a technique that comprises inhaling for four counts, holding the breath for seven counts, then exhaling for eight counts. To practice this method, sit comfortably and inhale deeply through your nostrils for four counts. Hold your breath for seven counts, then exhale gently through your mouth for eight counts. Repeat the cycle numerous times, focusing on your breathing rhythm and the sensation of profound relaxation in your body.

Muscle Relaxation in Stages

While progressive muscle relaxation is not strictly a breathing technique, it is frequently used in conjunction with deep breathing to induce deep relaxation in the body. Lay on your back or sit in a comfortable position to perform this technique. Tense each muscle group in your body for a few seconds, then release the tension and allow the muscle to relax, beginning with your toes. As you move up your body, tensing and relaxing each muscle group individually until you reach your head.

Integrating Guided Autogenic Training with Deep Breathing

Now that you know some ways for obtaining deep relaxation through breathing, it's time to include them into your Guided Autogenic Training practice. Deep breathing can be used to deepen your sense of calm and lower arousal during guided autogenic training. Here are some tips for incorporating deep breathing into your practice:

Begin your practice by taking a few deep breaths and concentrating on the sensation of your breath traveling in and out of your body.

Continue to focus on your breath as you progress through the stages of guided autogenic training, utilizing it as an anchor to bring your attention back to the present moment.

During the affirmations stage, aim to match your breath to the words you're saying, inhaling deeply as you utter the affirmation and expelling as you let go of any tension in your body.

When you reach the deep relaxation stage, continue to focus on your breath as a tool to deepen your relaxation and minimize excitement.

By including deep breathing into your Guided Autogenic Training practice, you may maximize the advantages of both and experience a greater sensation of relaxation and well-being.

Conclusion

Deep breathing is an important component of Guided Autogenic Training since it is a powerful tool for generating deep relaxation and lowering arousal. You can stimulate the parasympathetic nervous system and enhance feelings of relaxation and well-being by practicing techniques such as diaphragmatic breathing, box breathing, alternate nostril breathing, 4-7-8 breathing, and progressive muscle relaxation. When deep breathing is incorporated into your Guided Autogenic Training exercise, it can boost the benefits of the practice and help you experience a better sense of serenity and tranquility.

Chapter 3

Progressive Muscle Relaxation: A Step-by-Step Guide to Relieving Tension and Stress in Your Body

Progressive muscle relaxation (PMR) may be just what you need if you're seeking for a simple and effective technique to alleviate tension and stress in your body. PMR is a relaxation technique that involves tensing and relaxing certain muscle groups in your body, allowing you to become more aware of physical sensations and attain profound relaxation.

In this chapter, we'll look at the advantages of PMR, how it works, and how to use it successfully.

What exactly is Progressive Muscle Relaxation (PMR)?

Edmund Jacobson, a physician who thought that muscular tension was a main cause of anxiety and stress, developed progressive muscle relaxation in the 1920s. PMR is a technique that involves systematically tensing and relaxing certain muscle groups in your body one at a time.

You can become more aware of physiological sensations and achieve a state of profound relaxation by focusing your attention on each muscle group and purposefully tensing and relaxing them.

Advantages of Progressive Muscle Relaxation

Progressive muscular relaxation has numerous advantages, including:

Reduced Muscle Tension: PMR can help you release muscle tension and stress, lowering pain and suffering.

PMR is an excellent technique to prepare your body for sleep, and it can help you fall asleep sooner and remain asleep longer.

Reduced Anxiety: By relaxing your muscles and focusing your attention on your body, PMR can aid in the reduction of anxiety and the promotion of sensations of peace and relaxation.

Improved Mood: PMR can aid in the promotion of emotions of well-being and the improvement of your general mood.

What Is the Process of Progressive Muscle Relaxation?

PMR works by tensing and relaxing certain muscle groups in your body in a methodical manner. By tensing each muscle group on purpose, you increase blood flow to the area, making you more aware of the muscle and any stress or discomfort that may be there.

Then, by relaxing the muscle and releasing the tension, you can achieve deep relaxation in your body.

Step-by-Step Instructions for Progressive Muscle Relaxation

Now that you understand the benefits of PMR and how it works, let's look at a step-by-step guide to efficiently using this technique.

Locate a peaceful and comfortable location where you will not be disturbed. Lie on your back or take a seat in a comfy chair.

Take a few deep breaths, paying attention to how your breath moves in and out of your body. Allow yourself to settle into the environment.

Begin by tensing and pinching your toes for a few seconds. Then, relax your toes totally by releasing the tension.

Continue to your feet, tensing and holding the muscles in your feet for a few seconds. Then, relax your feet totally and remove the strain.

Continue working your way up your body, tensing and relaxing each muscle group individually. Concentrate on the sensation of tension in each muscle area, allowing yourself to let go and relax fully.

Then, tensing and relaxing each muscle group in turn, go on to your calves, thighs, and buttocks. Then, tensing and relaxing each muscle group in turn, go on to your belly, chest, and back.

Finally, alternate between tensing and relaxing your arms, shoulders, neck, and head. Allow yourself to feel entirely at ease and comfortable.

Progression Muscle Relaxation Techniques

Here are a few pointers to help you efficiently practice progressive muscle relaxation:

Practice on a daily basis: PMR is most effective when practiced on a regular basis, ideally every day.

Practice in a comfortable position: Whether lying down or sitting in a chair, it's critical to practice PMR in a comfortable position. Find a position in which you can fully relax your muscles.

To fully focus on your muscle groups and physiological sensations, it's essential to practice PMR in a peaceful and tranquil place where you won't be distracted.

Concentrate on the sensation of tension: As you tense each muscle group, concentrate on the sensation of tension in that place. This will assist you in becoming more aware of physiological sensations as well as promoting deeper relaxation.

utilize images: You can utilize imagery to help you relax when doing PMR. Imagine yourself in a quiet area, such as a beach or forest, and concentrate on the sounds and sensations of that environment.

Be patient: PMR is a method that requires practice and time to learn. Be patient with yourself and don't anticipate instant gratification.

Combine with other relaxation techniques: When paired with other relaxation techniques such as deep breathing, visualization, or meditation, PMR can be even more effective.

Conclusion

Progressive muscle relaxation is a simple and effective method for reducing body tension and stress, promoting deep relaxation, and improving general well-being. You can become more aware of physiological sensations and develop a sense of calm and relaxation by carefully tensing and relaxing each muscle group in your body.

Remember to practice on a regular basis, to concentrate on the tension, and to be patient with yourself as you learn this method. PMR can become a powerful tool for lowering stress and boosting overall health and well-being with time and practice.

Chapter 4

Visualizing Peace and Tranquility: Harnessing the Power of Your Imagination to Promote Deep Relaxation

Visualizing calm and tranquillity is an effective approach for achieving deep relaxation and reducing stress. It is utilizing your imagination to conjure up a mental image of a tranquil and calming setting, then concentrating on the details of that scenario to generate a sensation of calm and relaxation.

Visualization has been utilized for centuries in many spiritual and contemplative activities, and it has been proven to be a useful method for encouraging relaxation and stress reduction. Visualization has been found in studies to help alleviate anxiety, sadness, and chronic pain, as well as increase general well-being and quality of life.

In this chapter, we will look at how to utilize visualization to induce deep relaxation and stress reduction, as well as present a step-by-step approach to get you started.

Step 1: Locate a peaceful and comfortable location.

Find a peaceful and comfortable place where you won't be bothered to practice visualizing. Sit or lie down in a comfortable posture, and make sure your practice will not be disturbed.

Step 2: Select a serene and tranquil scene.

Select a tranquil and calming scene that speaks to you. This could be a beach, a forest, a mountain, or any other location that makes you feel at ease and peaceful. Consider imagining yourself in that location and visualizing the specifics of the scene.

Step 3: Use your senses.

Engage your senses and become immersed in the scene. Make a mental image of the area using all of your senses. What do you notice? What do you think you're hearing? What are you smelling? What are your thoughts? Your visualization will be more successful if it is vivid and detailed.

Step 4: Pay attention to your breathing.

Concentrate on your breathing while you imagine a serene scenario. Inhale slowly and deeply through your nose and exhale through your mouth. Feel the air moving in and out of your body as an anchor to keep you focused and comfortable.

Step 5: Maintain your focus.

Maintain your concentrate on your visualization. If your mind wanders, gently return it to the scene and re-engage your senses. Don't worry if staying concentrated is difficult at first; with experience, it will become easier.

Step 6: Bring your visualization to a close.

When you're ready to terminate your visualization, gradually return your attention to your physical surroundings. Open your eyes and take a few deep breaths. Take a time to notice how you're feeling and any changes in your physical or mental state.

Suggestions for Effective Visualization

Practice on a regular basis to reap the maximum benefits from visualization. Even a few minutes per day can have a significant impact.

Use positive affirmations: Use positive affirmations or words that reinforce your sense of peace and tranquillity to boost your visualization.

Make it your own: Make your visualization your own by personalizing it. Include things that reflect your personal experiences and tastes.

Visualize throughout the day: Use visualization to achieve relaxation and stress reduction throughout the day. Take a few minutes when you're feeling overwhelmed or nervous to envision your serene setting and focus on your breathing.

Conclusion

Visualizing calm and tranquillity is an effective approach for fostering deep relaxation and stress reduction. You can engage your senses and produce a sense of calm and relaxation by using your imagination to construct a mental picture of a quiet place. Remember to practice on a regular basis, to utilize positive affirmations, and to personalize your visualization.

Visualization, with time and effort, can become a helpful technique for boosting general health and well-being.

Chapter 5

Use imagery: As you practice PMR, you can also use imagery to enhance your relaxation. For example, imagine yourself in a peaceful setting, like a beach or forest, and focus on the sounds and sensations of that environment.

Progressive muscle relaxation (PMR) is a technique in which distinct muscle groups in the body are tensed and subsequently relaxed one at a time. It is an extremely effective approach for relieving tension and stress and encouraging relaxation. In this chapter, we'll look at how to use images to improve your PMR practice.

Imagery is the process of utilizing your imagination to generate a mental image of a tranquil and calming place. You can improve your relaxation and reduce tension by imagining a serene place. Imagine yourself in a beach or forest, for example, and focus on the sounds and sensations of that place to encourage relaxation and deeper levels of calm.

Here are some ideas for using imagery to improve your PMR practice:

Step 1: Select a tranquil location.

Choose a quiet environment that speaks to you. This could be a beach, a forest, a mountain, or any other location that makes you feel at ease and peaceful. Consider imagining yourself in that surroundings and visualizing the scene's features.

Step 2: Use your senses.

Engage your senses and become immersed in the scene. Make a mental image of the area using all of your senses. What do you notice? What do you think you're hearing? What are you smelling? What are your thoughts? Your visualization will be more successful if it is vivid and detailed.

Step 3: Align your imagery and muscle relaxation.

Coordination your images and muscle relaxation while you practice PMR. For example, as you tighten and then relax your muscles, imagine the tension leaving your body and sinking deeper into the serene environment you've created.

Step 4: Make use of positive affirmations.

Use positive affirmations or words that reinforce your sense of serenity and tranquillity to boost your visualization. You could, for example, tell yourself, "I am relaxed and at peace" or "I am calm and centered."

Step 5: Consistent practice

Practice imagery and PMR on a regular basis to get the most out of them. Even a few minutes per day can have a significant impact. You can improve your relaxation and reduce stress by including imagery into your PMR practice.

Advantages of Using Imagery with PMR

Imagery can enable you to relax more deeply and achieve deeper levels of serenity and peace.

Reduces stress: Using imagery to promote feelings of calm and tranquillity can assist to lessen tension and anxiety.

Improves overall well-being: By incorporating imagery into your PMR practice, you can promote overall well-being while also reducing the negative effects of stress on the body and mind.

Conclusion

Using imagery in conjunction with PMR can help you relax and manage stress more efficiently. You can engage your senses and produce a sensation of calm and relaxation by visualizing a tranquil and calming setting. Remember to combine your images with muscle relaxation, to employ positive affirmations, and to practice on a regular basis. With time and effort, visualization can develop into a useful tool for boosting general health and well-being.

Chapter 6

Achieving Mental Clarity and Focus: Techniques for Clearing Your Mind and Eliminating Distractions

It might be difficult to stay focused and clear-headed in today's fast-paced society. With so many diversions and demands on our time, it's easy to become disorganized and disoriented. There are, however, ways that can help you cleanse your mind and gain mental clarity and focus. In this chapter, we'll look at some of these approaches and how to apply them in your daily life.

Breathing With Intention

Mindful breathing is one of the simplest and most effective strategies to improve mental clarity and focus. Mindful breathing entails paying attention to your breath and returning your concentration to it anytime your mind wanders.

Find a quiet area to sit or lie down to practice mindful breathing. Close your eyes and inhale deeply, filling your lungs with air. Hold your breath for a few seconds before exhaling gently, letting the stress leave your body with each breath.

Concentrate on the sensation of air moving in and out of your body while you breathe. Take note of the rise and fall of your chest, as well as the sensation of air going through your nose and mouth. If your mind wanders, simply return your attention to your breath and continue to breathe attentively.

Meditation is another effective strategy for increasing mental clarity and focus. Meditation can take numerous forms, but the majority of them entail sitting silently and focusing your concentration on a certain object or mantra.

Find a quiet area to sit or lie down to begin meditating. Close your eyes and concentrate on your breath or a specific object, such as a candle or a work of art. If your mind wanders, simply return your attention to your breath or the thing.

Meditation, with consistent practice, can assist to quiet the mind and increase attention and concentration. It can also help to alleviate tension and anxiety while also promoting a sense of serenity and inner peace.

Walking with Intention

Another approach for clearing your mind and improving focus is mindful walking. Find a peaceful spot to stroll to practice mindful walking, such as a park or a quiet street. Concentrate on the sensation of your feet touching the ground and the movement of your body as you walk.

Try not to get caught up in the sights, sounds, and smells surrounding you. Return your attention to the sensation of walking and the movement of your body. If your mind wanders, simply bring it back to the present moment and continue walking consciously.

Clean Up Your Environment

Your surroundings can have a significant impact on your mental clarity and focus. It might be tough to focus and stay on task if your surrounds are cluttered and disorganized. Take some time to tidy your environment to increase your mental clarity.

Begin by removing anything you no longer require or utilize. Then, arrange your remaining possessions in a manner that makes sense to you. Maintain a clean and tidy workspace, and attempt to avoid any distractions, such as noisy coworkers or a messy desk.

Take Rest Periods

Taking frequent pauses during the day might also aid with mental clarity and attention. When you labor for lengthy periods of time without taking a break, your mind can grow exhausted and your focus can weaken.

Take brief breaks throughout the day to stay fresh and focused. Stretch, go for a walk outside, or do something else to help you relax and clear your mind. When you return to work, you'll feel revitalized and ready to tackle your chores with newfound vigor and vigor.

Conclusion

Maintaining mental clarity and attention is critical for remaining productive and reaching your goals. You may increase your mental clarity and stay focused and on task by adding practices like mindful breathing, meditation, mindful walking, cleaning your environment, and taking breaks into your daily routine.

It is critical to remember that these strategies require experience and patience. Don't be disheartened if you don't notice immediate benefits. Consistent practice is essential for attaining mental clarity and focus.

It's also crucial to realize that everyone's path to mental clarity and focus is unique. What works for one person might not work for the next. It's critical to try out several strategies and see what works best for you.

Incorporating these tactics into your regular routine can improve your overall well-being. They can increase your mental clarity and attention while also reducing tension and anxiety and promoting a sense of serenity and inner peace. Give them a shot and see how they go.

Chapter 7

Understanding and Overcoming Negative Thought Patterns: Strategies for Developing a Positive Mindset

Negative thought patterns are a major impediment for many persons attempting to develop a good mindset. These patterns can manifest themselves in a variety of ways, ranging from self-criticism and self-doubt to worry and anxiety about the future. They can be especially difficult to eradicate because they are frequently strongly ingrained in our thinking and might feel like second nature.

However, you can retrain your brain to think more positively and break negative thought habits. The first stage is to become aware of when negative thoughts originate and their impact on your attitude and conduct. When you've identified negative thinking patterns, you may start challenging them and replacing them with more positive, empowering beliefs.

Cognitive restructuring is an effective approach for overcoming unfavorable thought habits. This entails recognizing negative ideas and then questioning their validity by reviewing the evidence for and against them. For example, if you find yourself thinking, "I'll never be able to succeed in my career," you might confront this notion by recalling all of the moments in your career when you have successfully conquered problems.

Focusing on gratitude is another helpful method for establishing a positive mindset. You can redirect your emphasis from negative to positive thoughts by taking time each day to concentrate on the things you are grateful for. This can assist to build a sense of positivity and optimism, which can reduce stress and enhance well-being.

It's also crucial to be around positive people and places. Negative people and situations can exhaust you and perpetuate your negative mental habits. Positive people and situations, on the other hand, can be uplifting and serve to foster positive mental patterns.

Finally, it is critical to cultivate self-compassion. Self-criticism and self-doubt can often drive negative thought patterns. You may assist to break this cycle and build a more positive perspective by practicing self-compassion and treating oneself with care and understanding.

Finally, cultivating a positive mentality entails recognizing and conquering negative thought patterns. You may retrain your brain to think more positively and build a sense of inner peace and well-being by practicing cognitive restructuring, focusing on thankfulness, surrounding yourself with positivity, and practicing self-compassion.

Chapter 8

Mindfulness Meditation: Achieving Inner Peace and Tranquility Through Focused Attention

Through concentrated attention, mindfulness meditation is a powerful tool for developing inner peace and tranquillity. Bringing your attention to the present moment and monitoring your thoughts and sensations without judgment is the goal of this practice.

To begin, locate a peaceful area where you may comfortably sit for several minutes. Set a timer for 5-10 minutes to get started. To focus yourself, close your eyes and take a few deep breaths.

Next, pay attention to your breathing. Take note of how the air enters and exits your body. If your thoughts wander, gently bring them back to your breath.

As you continue to concentrate on your breathing, you may notice thoughts and sensations arise in your mind and body. Rather than becoming engrossed in these distractions, simply notice them objectively and restore your focus to your breath.

Mindfulness meditation, when practiced on a daily basis, can help to reduce stress and anxiety, increase attention and concentration, and generate a sense of serenity and inner peace. It can also aid in the development of self-awareness and insight, which can be beneficial in detecting and addressing harmful thought patterns and other barriers to inner calm.

One of the advantages of mindfulness meditation is that it may be practiced at any time and from any location. You may also incorporate mindfulness into regular activities like doing the dishes or going for a walk. You may create a sense of mindfulness and inner calm in all facets of your life by turning your complete attention to the present moment.

It's crucial to remember that mindfulness meditation is a discipline that takes time and patience to master. If your mind wanders or you feel uncomfortable or frustrated, simply observe these thoughts and sensations without judgment and restore your focus to your breath.

Mindfulness meditation can have a significant impact on your general well-being if you incorporate it into your daily practice. You may reduce stress and anxiety, enhance attention and concentration, and promote a greater sense of serenity and well-being in your life by fostering a sense of mindfulness and inner peace.

Chapter 9

Cultivating Gratitude and Appreciation: Techniques for Recognizing and Celebrating the Good Things in Your Life

Gratitude and gratitude are powerful feelings that can bring us joy and contentment. We can build a sense of happiness and satisfaction in our lives by focusing on the positive aspects of our life.

However, in the midst of a hectic and often chaotic lifestyle, it is easy to lose sight of the wonderful aspects of our existence. We may become fixated on the negative or take the good things for granted.

Cultivating thankfulness and appreciation is a discipline that entails focusing on the positive parts of our lives and noticing the nice things that we may otherwise ignore.

Keeping a gratitude notebook is an effective practice for building gratitude and appreciation. This entails spending a few minutes each day writing down three to five things for which you are grateful. These might be small things like a warm cup of coffee in the morning or a good talk with a friend, or they can be more substantial items like a new career or a supportive family.

Focusing on the present moment is another strategy for generating gratitude and appreciation. You may appreciate the minor joys of life, such as the warmth of the sun on your skin or the sound of birds singing outdoors, by bringing your complete focus to the present moment.

You can also cultivate gratitude and appreciation by expressing gratitude to those around you. Whether it's a sincere thank-you email to a coworker or a simple remark to a friend, expressing gratitude can help to develop connections and foster a sense of connection and community.

Finally, remember that fostering thankfulness and appreciation is a practice that, like any other, requires time and work to develop. Set a consistent time each day to reflect on gratitude and appreciation, such as during your morning coffee or before going to bed.

Including thankfulness and appreciation in your daily life can have a significant impact on your overall well-being. By concentrating on the positive aspects of your life, you can build a sense of contentment and satisfaction, which can help to alleviate tension and anxiety and foster a greater sense of serenity and happiness.

Chapter 10

Applying Guided Autogenic Training in Your Daily Life: Incorporating These Mindfulness Techniques Into Your Daily Routine for Lasting Results.

Guided Autogenic Training approaches can be extremely effective tools for lowering stress, inducing relaxation, and fostering a stronger sense of peace and tranquillity.

However, in order to genuinely profit from these approaches, you must adopt them into your daily life in a durable and successful manner.

Setting up a specified period each day for practice is one approach to incorporate Guided Autogenic Training into your regular life. This can be as little as 10 minutes each day, but consistency is essential if you want to see long-term improvements.

It may be beneficial to your practice to provide a calming environment, such as a quiet room with soft lighting and comfy chairs. You can also integrate calming items, such as scented candles or soothing music, into your practice.

Another method to include Guided Autogenic Training into your regular life is to use it when you are stressed or anxious. If you're feeling overloaded at work, for example, you can take a few minutes to focus on your breathing and employ progressive muscle relaxation to relax your muscles.

You may also add Guided Autogenic Training into your daily practice by employing mindfulness techniques while performing everyday tasks. You can, for example, concentrate on your breathing while doing the dishes or walking to work, or you can utilize visualization techniques to visualize a serene setting when stopped in traffic.

Finally, keep in mind that the benefits of Guided Autogenic Training are cumulative, which means that the more you practice, the higher the benefits you will experience. You can build a stronger sense of peace and well-being by implementing these practices into your daily routine, which can have a significant impact on your overall quality of life.

To summarize, Guided Autogenic Training approaches have the ability to greatly improve your overall well-being by lowering stress, encouraging relaxation, and creating a stronger sense of calm and tranquillity. By adopting these techniques into your daily routine, you may create a long-term practice that will help you manage with daily stressors and foster a greater sense of contentment and fulfillment.

Printed in Great Britain
by Amazon